IN THIS ISSUE:

I0478827

tourism.com TATTLER

ISSUE 12 DECEMBER 2016

PUBLISHER
Tourism Tattler (Pty) Ltd.
PO Box 891, Umhlanga Rocks, 4320
KwaZulu-Natal, South Africa.
Website: www.tourismtattler.com

EXECUTIVE EDITOR Des Langkilde
Cell: +27 (0)82 374 7260
Fax: +27 (0)86 651 8080
E-mail: editor@tourismtattler.com
Skype: tourismtattler

MAGAZINE ADVERTISING
ADVERTISING DIRECTOR Bev Langkilde
Cell: +27 (0)71 224 9971
Fax: +27 (0)86 656 3860
E-mail: bev@tourismtattler.com
Skype: bevtourismtattler

SUBSCRIPTIONS
http://eepurl.com/bocIdD

BACK ISSUES (Click on the covers below).

▼ NOV 2016   ▼ OCT 2016   ▼ SEP 2016
  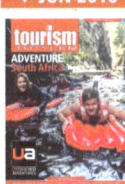

▼ AUG 2016   ▼ JUL 2016   ▼ JUN 2016

▼ MAY 2016   ▼ APR 2016   ▼ MAR 2016

▼ FEB 2016   ▼ JAN 2016   ▼ DEC 2015

CONTENTS

Front cover image courtesy of Lalibela Private Game Reserve

EDITORIAL CONTRIBUTORS

Adv. Louis Nel   Jean Francois Mourier
Bonnie Feldman   Lee-Ann Collingridge
Charley Ne   Lise Manley
Fiona Leppan   Martin Janse van Vuuren
Hannelie du Toit   Waverly J Hanson

MAGAZINE SPONSORS

ACCREDITATION

Official Travel Trade Journal and Media Partner to:

The Africa Travel Association (ATA)

Tel: +1 212 447 1357 • Email: _info@africatravelassociation.org_ • Website: _www.africatravelassociation.org_

ATA is a division of the Corporate Council on Africa (CCA), and a registered non-profit trade association in the USA, with headquarters in Washington, DC and chapters around the world. ATA is dedicated to promoting travel and tourism to Africa and strengthening intra-Africa partnerships. Established in 1975, ATA provides services to both the public and private sectors of the industry.

The African Travel & Tourism Association (Atta)

Tel: +44 20 7937 4408 • Email: _info@atta.travel_ • Website: _www.atta.travel_

Members in 22 African countries and 37 worldwide use Atta to: Network and collaborate with peers in African tourism; Grow their online presence with a branded profile; Ask and answer specialist questions and give advice; and Attend key industry events.

National Accommodation Association of South Africa (NAA-SA)

Tel: +27 86 186 2272 • Fax: +2786 225 9858 • Website: _www.naa-sa.co.za_

The NAA-SA is a network of mainly smaller accommodation providers around South Africa – from B&Bs in country towns offering comfortable personal service to luxurious boutique city lodges with those extra special touches – you're sure to find a suitable place, and at the same time feel confident that your stay at an NAA-SA member's establishment will meet your requirements.

Regional Tourism Organisation of Southern Africa (RETOSA)

Tel: +27 11 315 2420/1 • Fax: +27 11 315 2422 • Website: _www.retosa.co.za_

RETOSA is a Southern African Development Community (SADC) institution responsible for tourism growth and development. RETOSA's aims are to increase tourist arrivals to the region through. RETOSA Member States are Angola, Botswana, DR Congo, Lesotho, Madagascar, Malawi, Mauritius, Mozambique, Namibia, Seychelles, South Africa, Swaziland, Tanzania, Zambia and Zimbabwe.

Southern African Vehicle Rental and Leasing Association (SAVRALA)

Contact: _manager@savrala.co.za_ • Website: _www.savrala.co.za_

Founded in the 1970's, SAVRALA is the representative voice of Southern Africa's vehicle rental, leasing and fleet management sector. Our members have a combined national footprint with more than 600 branches countrywide. SAVRALA are instrumental in steering industry standards and continuously strive to protect both their members' interests, and those of the public, and are therefore widely respected within corporate and government sectors.

Seychelles Hospitality & Tourism Association (SHTA)

Tel: +248 432 5560 • Fax: +248 422 5718 • Website: _www.shta.sc_

The Seychelles Hospitality and Tourism Association was created in 2002 when the Seychelles Hotel Association merged with the Seychelles Hotel and Guesthouse Association. SHTA's primary focus is to unite all Seychelles tourism industry stakeholders under one association in order to be better prepared to defend the interest of the industry and its sustainability as the pillar of the country's economy.

Tourism, Hotel Investment and Networking Conference 2016

Website: _www.thincafrica.hvsconferences.com_

THINC Africa 2016 takes place in Cape Town from 6-7 September.

International Coalition of Tourism Partners (ICTP)

Website: _www.tourismpartners.org_

ICTP is a travel and tourism coalition of global destinations committed to Quality Services and Green Growth.

International Institute for Peace through Tourism

Website: _www.iipt.org_

IIPT is dedicated to fostering tourism initiatives that contribute to international understanding and cooperation.

World Travel Market

WTM Africa - Cape Town in April, WTM Latin America - São Paulo in April, and WTM - London in November. WTM is the place to do business.

The Safari Awards

Website: _www.safariawards.com_

Safari Award finalists are amongst the top 3% in Africa and the winners are unquestionably the best.

World Luxury Hotel Awards

Website: _www.luxuryhotelawards.com_

World Luxury Hotel Awards is an international company that provides award recognition to the best hotels from all over the world.

BEST DESIGN HOTEL IN

South Africa, Stellenbosch; CAPE Winelands luxury small hotel destination **Majeka House & Spa** has scooped a coveted international award in recognition of their world class interior design.

By **Lise Manley.**

Already a recipient of a string of awards and accolades over the years, Majeka House & Spa has clinched **Best Design Hotel in Africa & the Middle East** at the Condé Nast Johansens Awards for Excellence 2017.

Praised as a 'wining, dining and super styling destination', the award comes at the end of a successful and exciting year; owners Lloyd van der Merwe and Karine Dequeker-van der Merwe have been working on various upgrades and tweaks since last year, calling in the expertise of designer Etienne Hanekom to work on the hotel's rooms, Makaron Restaurant as well as the photogenic MLounge.

"So many international hotels look the same as each other and offer more of the same, we're just so pleased that both critics and guests recognise that different can be exciting without compromising on quality", says Lloyd.

For visitors to the Winelands, five-star Majeka House & Spa is a very attractive prospect indeed. From its perfect position near the historic town of Stellenbosch to a welcoming and intimate atmosphere, gourmet spoils at Makaron Restaurant by Pete Goffe-Wood, the boutique Majeka House Spa and of course, its on trend designer surrounds, it's a full house of luxury offerings and arresting eye candy at this 23-roomed Stellenbosch bolthole.

For bookings: +27 21 880 1549 or reservations@majekahouse.co.za

AFRICA & MIDDLE EAST

A fitting finale to the recent refurbishment is the launch of the hotel's newly redecorated Pool Rooms. The duo of designtastic suites is perched in front of a slick, shared heated pool and elegant terrace. Designed to complement one another while retaining their own identity, each of the suites has a distinct personality, brought to life beautifully by Hanekom.

"We already had such a wonderful response to Etienne's brave décor scheme in the rest of the hotel that we asked him to work more of his magic in these rooms which are two of our most popular offerings", says owner Lloyd who together with Karine has been hosting guests from around the world since 2008.

With an oversized flamingo print in the hotel's dining room proving a major talking point since the refurbishment of public areas was completed, Etienne extended the exotic bird reference in the rooms – making bold colour, pattern and design statements in each and making sure to include framed vintage prints of birds as a point of reference.

"It all started with a collection of vintage Audubon bird prints which we found and we took it from there", explains Etienne, "in nature, a riot of colour is often the norm, especially with birds, and I wanted to reflect that with the palette and furnishings so there are lots of

different textures, there's old, there's new and there's an out there colour palette too".

The first suite features a flamboyant marriage of coral and chartreuse, sumptuous fabrics and a mix of antique and contemporary furnishings while the adjacent suite includes swathes of emerald green coupled with oversized tropical scenes and a feature wall dressed in an on-trend, metallic geometric wallpaper. The result is a thoroughly opulent albeit playful atmosphere.

As with the rest of the facilities at Majeka House & Spa, no stone has been left unturned in the quest to provide a five-star experience in the Pool Rooms. From in-room coffee machines to impressive mini bars, there's no denying that luxury that oozes personality is the name of the game here. It's no surprise either that leisure and business travellers alike are more than thrilled to call Majeka House & Spa their home from home in the historic Winelands area.

A wise person once said that one should never check into a hotel that isn't as nice or nicer than one's own home. With it's out there decorative details and extensive menu of luxe offerings, not to mention the outstanding service, Majeka House & Spa offers much more than that and then some.

ICONIC SAFARI LODGES

Africa Albida Tourism's luxurious properties, located in two of Southern Africa's iconic destinations – Victoria Falls, **Zimbabwe**, and Chobe, **Botswana** – are featured in this month's **Africa Adventure Travel GeoDirectory**.

The properties encapsulate the very essence of Africa, and provide the perfect setting for that unforgettable holiday.

Africa Albida Tourism, a prominent Zimbabwean hospitality group, prides itself on being a regional leader in sustainable tourism, ensuring that the local communities and the environment benefit from its operations.

#1 Victoria Falls Safari Lodge

Voted the Best Safari Lodge/Resort Hotel in Zimbabwe for 20 consecutive years by the Association of Zimbabwe Travel Agents, Victoria Falls Safari Lodge is located just 4km from one of the Seven Natural Wonders of the World.

Built on a plateau, the sunset-facing Victoria Falls Safari Lodge offers stunning views of pristine bushveld, including a large central waterhole frequented by elephant, buffalo and other wildlife.

Built of thatch and timber, the lodge rises several levels, giving the impression of a vast open-plan tree house, with the authentic African feel extending to all 72 rooms, which face outwards to the wilds.

View this listing HERE.

#2 Victoria Falls Safari Club

The premium 20-room Victoria Falls Safari Club, set alongside the Victoria Falls Safari Lodge, offers guests exclusivity and the very best of Africa in ultimate luxury.

Built high on a plateau which forms the natural boundary to the Zambezi National Park, Victoria Falls Safari Club offers spacious accommodation with uninterrupted views of unspoilt bushveld, spectacular African sunsets and wildlife.

It has its own private lounge and viewing deck where guests may enjoy complimentary head, neck and shoulder massages, afternoon tea and pastries, sundowners and canapés and seasonal edutainment presentations.

View this listing HERE.

AFRICA ALBIDA
T O U R I S M

#3 Victoria Falls Safari Suites

The six spacious two and three-bedroom Victoria Falls Safari Suites, ideal for families, small groups and couples seeking space, privacy and comfort, can accommodate up to five and seven people respectively.

Set in a natural bush environment in the magnificent grounds of Victoria Falls Safari Lodge resort, the split-level Safari Suites overlook a small private waterhole, which attracts bushbuck, warthog and a rich variety of birds.

All bedrooms are ensuite, and each Safari Suite has a lounge with floor-to-ceiling sliding doors opening onto a patio. The lounge features a courtesy counter which includes a fridge, microwave and sink. A TV lounge with a sofa bed, recommended for a child under 12 years, is located adjacent to the main lounge.

 *View this listing* HERE*.*

#4 Lokuthula Lodges

Lokuthula Lodges are the highest quality and best located self-catering units in the Victoria Falls area.

The self-catering two- and three-bedroom lodges, which may also be booked on a bed and breakfast basis, are split-level and have one or two bathrooms, a lounge and terrace, a fully equipped kitchen and braai area.

Each of the 31 lodges has two sofa beds in the lounge, allowing up to six people to be accommodated in the two-bedroom lodges, and eight in the three-bedroom lodges.

Located in the grounds of the Victoria Falls Safari Lodge resort, the lodges overlook indigenous bush allowing guests to enjoy sightings of warthog, bushbuck and a rich variety of birds from their private terrace.

View this listing HERE*.*

#5 The Boma

The Boma – Dinner & Drum Show is a "must-do" Victoria Falls experience, and offers an unforgettable African fusion of mouth-watering local cuisine, spirited dance performances, interactive drumming, and traditional storytelling.

The Boma, also located in the grounds of the Victoria Falls Safari Lodge resort, provides a unique cultural experience that bombards the senses with the tastes, sights and sounds of Africa.

The four-course meal includes a starter platter, soup from the campfire, a braai (barbecue) buffet (where no plate is complete without the famous warthog steak), and dessert, with the evening's festivities being rounded off with an energising interactive drumming show.

#6 Ngoma Safari Lodge

Located on the edge of Botswana's Chobe National Park, home to the largest herds of elephants on Earth, the luxurious Ngoma Safari Lodge, recently described in The United Kingdom's Town & Country magazine as possibly "the finest safari lodge in Africa", is an oasis in a wildlife wonderland.

This boutique eight-suite lodge offers unrivalled panoramic views over the game-rich Chobe River and floodplain, where there is the opportunity to view the famous Chobe elephants, buffalo, and migrating zebra.

Activities include an all-day safari, made up of a cruise on the Chobe River (where guests may see the iconic sight of elephants swimming trunks up as they cross the river), a picnic lunch and a game drive through Chobe National Park, guided walks and night and day game drives.

View this listing HERE.

Market Intelligence Report

SATSA
Southern Africa Tourism Services Association

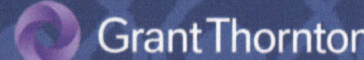
Grant Thornton

The information below was extracted from data available as at **01 December 2016**. By **Martin Jansen van Vuuren** of **Grant Thornton**.

ARRIVALS

The latest available data from **Statistics South Africa** is for **January to September 2016***:

	Current period	Change over same period last year
UK	314 596	11.4%
Germany	197 248	21.2%
USA	259 274	18.6%
India	73 902	58.1%
China (incl Hong Kong)	88 997	26.6%
Overseas Arrivals	1 770 568	19.5%
African Arrivals	5 639 842	12.9%
Total Foreign Arrivals	7 418 751	14.3%

HOTEL STATS

The latest available data from **STR Global** is for **January to October 2016**:

Current period	Average Room Occupancy (ARO)	Average Room Rate (ARR)	Revenue Per Available Room (RevPAR)
All Hotels in SA	64.5%	R 1 155	R 745
All 5-star hotels in SA	65.1%	R 2 115	R 1 376
All 4-star hotels in SA	64.1%	R 1 069	R 685
All 3-star hotels in SA	64.8%	R 915	R 593
Change over same period last year			
All Hotels in SA	3.0%	8.9%	12.1%
All 5-star hotels in SA	5.1%	10.8%	16.4%
All 4-star hotels in SA	3.8%	6.5%	10.6%
All 3-star hotels in SA	3.3%	6.2%	9.7%

ACSA DATA

The latest available data from **ACSA** is for **October 2016**:

Change over same period last year	Passengers arriving on International Flights	Passengers arriving on Regional Flights	Passengers arriving on Domestic Flights
OR Tambo International	2.9%	4.4%	5.5%
Cape Town International	13.6%	22.6%	6.3%
King Shaka International	20.9%	N/A	8.9%

CAR RENTAL DATA

The latest available data from **SAVRALA** is for **January to June 2015**:

	Current period	Change over same period last year
Industry rental days	8 139 127	-1%
Industry utilisation	70.2%	-0.7%
Industry Average daily revenue	2 498 944 728	1%

WHAT THIS MEANS FOR MY BUSINESS

The data continues to indicate the recovery of international arrivals from 2015 as reflected in the growth in Stats SA foreign arrival data, growth in the rates of 5-star hotels and growth in the arrivals on international and regional flights. The domestic tourism market has also grown as reflected in the growth in the rates of 3-star hotels and arrivals on domestic flights. The growth in foreign tourism is partially driven by the decline in the Rand exchange rate and the tourism industry is cautioned to build their competitive advantage on quality and service rather than depend on a depreciating exchange rates. 🅣

*Note that African Arrivals plus Overseas Arrivals do not add to Total Foreign Arrivals due to the exclusion of unspecified arrivals, which could not be allocated to either African or Overseas.

For more information contact Martin at Grant Thornton on +27 (0)21 417 8838 or visit: http://www.gt.co.za

The Right Mindset For Running
Your Own Business

By **Waverly J Hanson.**

Running a business is a big challenge. Even the most modest enterprise takes hard work and dedication to thrive. If you own your own business, approaching it with the right frame of mind is vital to your long-term success. Here's an overview of where your head needs to be if you want to build your business into something great.

Choose Your Goals And Strive For Them

The best part of being a successful business owner is that you get to define "successful" however you want. Do you want to make a certain amount of money? Serve a certain number of customers? Operate throughout a certain region? Maybe you'd prefer to pursue less traditional definitions of the term. There's nothing wrong with cutting your profits to provide better benefits to your employees if that's something you've chosen to do. What really matters, in the end, is that you should be reaching for goals you define yourself, not those established by others.

Once you have your goals laid out, the hard work of figuring out how to achieve them begins. In order to do this properly, you have to let go of your fear of failure. Running a business is such a complicated process that

the odds of you never making a mistake are virtually zero. Understand that not every step will take you towards your goal. Once you realize you have erred, take your experience as a learning opportunity and refocus on how to achieve your goals again.

Pull Talent Close To Yourself

Exceptionally few businesses succeed based on the efforts of a single individual, no matter how brilliant they might be. Even an artisanal craftsman who works alone relies on good suppliers and toolmakers to provide the raw materials he needs. Recognize that leadership is a key part of running your business and aim to surround yourself with other talented people who will share your goals.

Attracting the sort of talented and hard-working people you need to succeed is not just about paying good salaries. Devote a portion of your working hours to making sure that your employees feel satisfied and successful in their work. Cultivate the skills of your team members and trust them with responsibility when they are ready for it. Pay attention to what your employees have to say and remember that as your business grows, they will end up being more familiar with its inner workings than you are.

Obsess Over Quality, Not Process

Many people would say that obsession is a positive quality when it is turned to constructive ends and this is definitely true when it comes to running a business. You will probably be inspired to put in long hours and lots of thought to nurture your business. Make sure you are spending your attention on the right thing, which is the quality of the products or services your business delivers.

While there is nothing wrong with trying to make your business more efficient, you shouldn't ever let process improvements come at the expense of quality. Ultimately, what you do for your customers is what defines your business. Make sure you are always producing something you can be proud of and the processes required to produce it will fall into place.

There is no one road map to creating a successful business. Every owner who is satisfied with his or her business probably defines success differently. Despite the diversity of definitions available out there, certain attitudes are common to every successful business owner. Cultivate the right mindset for your work and you make your business a success too.

About the Author: Waverly J. Hanson *is a licensed professional counselor, licensed marriage coach, military and family life consultant, professional trainer and author of How to Divorce-Proof Your Marriage. She has more than 25 years of experience helping individuals and couples improve their lives. For more information visit PersonalDevelopmentGoals.mywebpal.com*

Market Access
for South African
SMEs

South African Tourism has partnered with the Southern African Tourism Services Association (SATSA) on a brand-new market access partnership to develop the Small & Medium Enterprise (SME) tourism sector whilst contributing towards transformation.

By **Hannelie du Toit**.

Based on the premise that innovation is the key to bringing Historically Disadvantaged Enterprises (HDEs) into the mainstream of tourism and the understanding that transformation initiatives must first make commercial sense, the Market Access Programme is an intermediate marketplace where carefully selected and prepared emerging product get to meet with large trade members in an environment that allows for informed discussions and business deals. The project is based on learnings from the very successful Gauteng SME market access event SATSA hosted in March 2016, in partnership with the Gauteng Tourism Authority, Jo'burg Tourism, South African Tourism, the Gauteng Enterprise Propeller and the Gauteng Department of Economic Development.

Running between December 2016 and May 2017, the initiative will see small- and medium-sized historically disadvantaged enterprises from across the country participate, through a graduated selection process, in training and peer-to-peer mentorship. This will be followed by directly introducing selected SMEs to key decision makers from the leading inbound tourism trade at a speed marketing session to be hosted on 15 May 2017, the day before the annual Tourism INDABA in Durban as part of South African Tourism's Hidden Gems programme. This will culminate in the selected SMEs exhibiting at the trade show from the 16th to 18th of May.

Historically disadvantaged small- and medium-sized tourism businesses across South Africa are invited to register before 15 December 2016.

Through an inclusive selection process, a committee will select 30 trade relevant SME products per province who will then attend a 5-day training course and finally the top 10 products per province will be selected to participate in peer-to-peer mentorship and trade marketing platforms.

Provincial and local tourism authorities and other interested parties are invited to join the project by participating in the selection committee to ensure that the best of the best small businesses advance through the process and by attending the various workshops, and assisting selected SMEs.

Recognising that the inbound tour operator plays a pivotal role in facilitating interactions with SMEs, members of SATSA will be approached to offer their services as mentors, present at provincial training programmes and to attend the one-day speed marketing session on 15 May 2017.

The industry plays a large role in providing candid feedback and helpful critique directly to the SMEs to improve their individual products.

About the Author: Hannelie du Toit is the Industry Self-Regulation Manager at the Southern Africa Tourism Services Association (SATSA). For more information contact Hannelie on +27 083 600 3555 or email Hannelie@satsa.co.za

The winning 'Like' or 'Share' during the month of **December 2016** will receive **2 Kenyan Scarfs** with the compliments of **Livingstones Supply Co** – *Suppliers of the Finest Products to the Hospitality Industry*.

'Like' / 'Share' / 'Connect' with these Social Media icons to win!

Livingston Supply Company

TourismTattler

Competition Rules: Only one winner will be selected each month on a random selection draw basis. The prize winner will be notified via social media. The prize will be delivered by the sponsor to the winners postal address within South Africa. Should the winner reside outside of South Africa, delivery charges may be applicable. The prize may not be exchanged for cash.

Beautiful scarf made from 100% Viscose, 35 x 160cm. Produced locally from imported fabric in a range of exquisitely woven patterns. The vibrant and rich as well soft and muted colours reflecting the beauty and ethnicity of the African nature and culture. These may be worn to temper the evening or morning chill or to keep cool in the African sun. Adding elegance, style, comfort and functionality to any wardrobe.

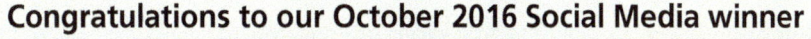

Congratulations to our October 2016 Social Media winner

@PlettGameRes

Plett Game Reserve offers Big-5 Game Drives, Horse Safaries, and Accommodation in Plettenberg Bay, Garden Route, South Africa. **Plett Game Reserve** will receive **2 CDs**: **1x Essential South African Jazz** (the Jo'burg sessions) **CD** *plus* **1x Songs & Stories of Africa CD** with the compliments of **Livingstones Supply Co** – *Suppliers of the Finest Products to the Hospitality Industry*.

For more information visit *www.livingstonessupplyco.co.za*

Exploring Game Capacity in Big 5 Reserves

Ever wondered why some game reserves have more Big Five sightings than others? This article provides the answers.

By **Des Langkilde**.

According to Vernon Wait, owner of South African based tour operator Pembury Tours, who specialise in safaris to some of southern Africa's premium Big Five game reserves: *"The three main aspects of any African safari are the game-viewing, the accommodation and the food, but the main reason why tourists go on safari is to view game and, as an inbound industry, we should try to remember this as there is sometimes a risk that we allow other, less significant, factors to determine where we send our clients for their safari experience."*

This statement published in the August edition of Tourism Tattler piqued my curiosity *(read the article here)*. Do some game reserves provide more Big Five sighting opportunities than others? And if so, why?

Cramming a lot of game into a confined area would ensure frequent sightings of different game species, but tourists don't travel to Africa to visit a zoo and, also, tourists want to know that they are on safari where the game viewing is sustainable. They come to experience Africa's wildlife roaming free in their natural habitat - specifically the Big Five (Cape buffalo, elephant, leopard, and rhinoceros).

But wildlife husbandry and conservation is not that simple, specifically when predators, plains game and large herbivores are confined by fences and endemic flora biodiversity. Issues such as the game carrying capacity and grazing suitability of the land, the migratory instincts of certain species, the potential spread of diseases, and the fundamental role that grazing animals have in the dispersion of plant seeds are just a few of the considerations that wildlife conservation managers are faced with.

For answers to these issues, I turned to Rob Gradwell, Managing Director of Lalibela Private Game Reserve in South Africa's malaria-free Eastern Cape province.

"The fact that Lalibela has the densest population of free-roaming predators in the Eastern Cape, is directly attributable to the substantial areas of savannah grassland – the vegetation type with the highest carrying capacity for herbivore grazing – that we are fortunate to have on Lalibela.

"This is a very significant asset because it means that Lalibela is able to sustain vast herds of plains game, which in turn determines the number of predators that we can sustain on the reserve.

"To put it to you another way, if every hectare of the valley bushveld biome can sustain X number of grazers like impala, and every hectare of savannah grassland can sustain 10 times X, then two facts become clear:
1. On a sustainable basis, significantly more predators can exist on properties that have large areas of savannah grassland than on properties that do not have much savannah grassland, and;
2. Since predators have significantly more game to prey on over savannah grassland than other biomes, there are far better opportunities for guests to see both predators and prey.

"Regarding the game carrying capacity and grazing suitability of the land, we commissioned a team of game management experts whose analysis determined the ideal numbers of various species of game that the reserve can sustain, which is based on the five flora biomes found here.

" In addition, the new owners of Lalibela acquired more land in late July 2016 to expand the boundaries of the reserve, which now stretches over 10,255 hectares *(over 25,000 acres)*. So based on the game carrying capacity analysis, we embarked on a game repopulation programme *(read more on this aspect here)*, with significant purchases of

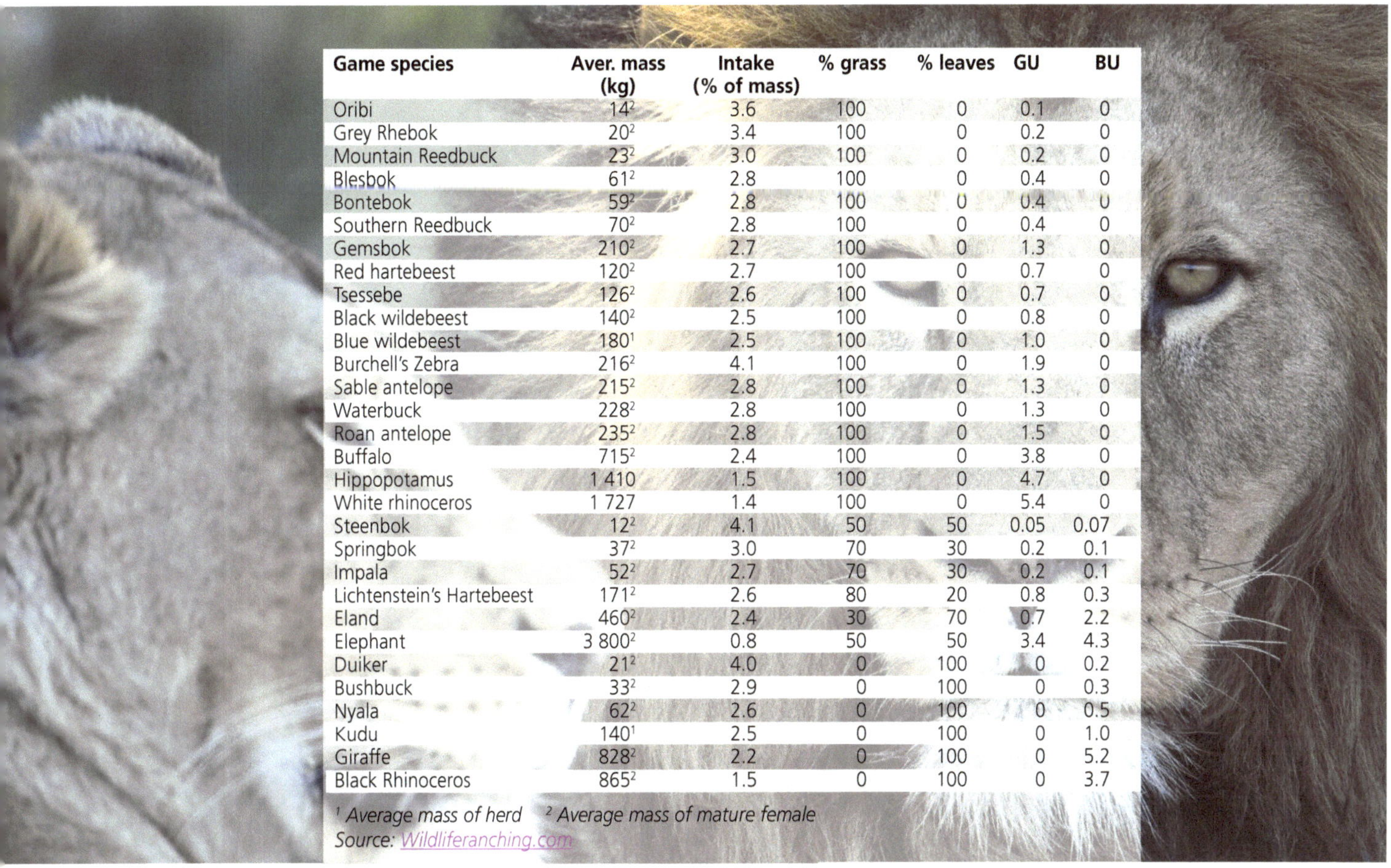

Game species	Aver. mass (kg)	Intake (% of mass)	% grass	% leaves	GU	BU
Oribi	14[2]	3.6	100	0	0.1	0
Grey Rhebok	20[2]	3.4	100	0	0.2	0
Mountain Reedbuck	23[2]	3.0	100	0	0.2	0
Blesbok	61[2]	2.8	100	0	0.4	0
Bontebok	59[2]	2.8	100	0	0.4	0
Southern Reedbuck	70[2]	2.8	100	0	0.4	0
Gemsbok	210[2]	2.7	100	0	1.3	0
Red hartebeest	120[2]	2.7	100	0	0.7	0
Tsessebe	126[2]	2.6	100	0	0.7	0
Black wildebeest	140[2]	2.5	100	0	0.8	0
Blue wildebeest	180[1]	2.5	100	0	1.0	0
Burchell's Zebra	216[2]	4.1	100	0	1.9	0
Sable antelope	215[2]	2.8	100	0	1.3	0
Waterbuck	228[2]	2.8	100	0	1.3	0
Roan antelope	235[2]	2.8	100	0	1.5	0
Buffalo	715[2]	2.4	100	0	3.8	0
Hippopotamus	1 410	1.5	100	0	4.7	0
White rhinoceros	1 727	1.4	100	0	5.4	0
Steenbok	12[2]	4.1	50	50	0.05	0.07
Springbok	37[2]	3.0	70	30	0.2	0.1
Impala	52[2]	2.7	70	30	0.2	0.1
Lichtenstein's Hartebeest	171[2]	2.6	80	20	0.8	0.3
Eland	460[2]	2.4	30	70	0.7	2.2
Elephant	3 800[2]	0.8	50	50	3.4	4.3
Duiker	21[2]	4.0	0	100	0	0.2
Bushbuck	33[2]	2.9	0	100	0	0.3
Nyala	62[2]	2.6	0	100	0	0.5
Kudu	140[1]	2.5	0	100	0	1.0
Giraffe	828[2]	2.2	0	100	0	5.2
Black Rhinoceros	865[2]	1.5	0	100	0	3.7

[1] Average mass of herd   [2] Average mass of mature female
Source: Wildliferanching.com

Cape buffalo, black wildebeest, zebra, kudu, giraffe, impala, and blesbok, which have been introduced to both the 'Big-5 area' as well as in the new breeding area. The existing herds of elephant and hippo are breeding well and their numbers are still within the sustainable carrying capacity of the reserve.

"Our long term project aimed at eradicating alien invasive plant species and to re-establish the endemic flora within the reserve is still ongoing *(read more about this project here)*, and will ultimately create still more grassland savannah to sustain the plains game and hence the predator species such as lion, cheetah, leopard, and the smaller cats like serval, caracal, and black footed cats. Then there's the scavenger species who clean up after them such as hyena, aardwolf, foxes and jackal, which are also breeding in sustainable numbers," says Gradwell.

According to research* undertaken by the Department of Animal, Wildlife and Grassland Sciences, University of the Free State, the basic requirement of management systems for sustainable game production from temperate savannah or veld is to balance the stocking rate of the various game species with the grazing and browsing capacity of the savannah biome.

The study cites a rather complicated formula for determining the carrying capacity of African savannah for large ungulates (over 100 kg in mass), which takes into account the type of grass (sweetveld or sourveld), the chemical defences of woody plants (nutritional characteristics of leaves in different phenological stages), and the effects of soil type, and frequency of precipitation and fire. To complicate matters further, the agricultural method for measuring the metabolic mass of animals such as cows and sheep in terms of Animal Units (AU) and Large Stock Units (LSU) had to be adjusted to account for the ecological separation of herbivore game species.

Using the above table, the author then delves into two calculation formulae for determining the grazing capacity per hectare versus the browsing capacity, and then advises an even more sophisticated calculation approach to adjust the browse capacity at peak biomass for a reduction in browse availability during each month of the year according to specific values. This is a complicated science but it does give some insight to the reader as to why the game viewing experience can differ so drastically from one property to the next.

Lions on Lalibela Private Game Reserve

Anti-Poaching: To Rescue

While on a game drive through a private reserve in Northern KwaZulu-Natal, our tour group spotted two animals that had fallen victim to poaching snares. Both were still alive and lumbering through the bush in obvious pain and agony. What would the standard procedure be - to sedate the animal, remove the snare and treat its wounds or to shoot and put the animal out of its misery?

By **Des Langkilde**.

Understandably, such a decision would be based on the severity of the animal's wounds but surely any effort that would increase its chance of survival would be worth the effort? However, such decisions are rarely as simple as they seem. Given the following scenario, how would you have handled the situation?

The first animal, a male Impala, had a strangle-noose wire wrapped around its neck with the lead wide entangled around its rear legs. As the Impala moves, the noose tightens and ensures a slow, agonising death by strangulation. No bleeding around the neck was evident and the Impala continued to graze, which seemed to indicate that he had not been snared too long ago.

The second animal, a Blue Wildebeest, had its front left elbow joint almost severed from a wire snare and, judging by the lack of bleeding around the area, must have endured the pain for several hours, if not days.

The time of the Impala sighting at around 3:30 pm left enough daylight for a rescue operation to be undertaken, while the Wildebeest was spotted less than 500m away from the Impala sighting at around 5pm.

Here's what actually happened: the very competent (but clearly powerless) safari guide radioed the lodge manager, who arrived at the first sighting with an assistant lodge manager some 10 minutes later. After casually observing the distressed Impala, lodge manager one stated that it would need to be put-down as it was "pumping blood" which was clearly not the case.

After asking if they could not sedate the Impala and at least attempt a rescue, the assistant lodge manager got decidedly authoritative, stating "We don't allow tourists or media to witness this type of situation!" And off we were sent to continue the game drive - only to encounter the poor Wildebeest, which said competent guide again reported-in.

Now the last thing that any lodge manager should tell a journalist is to "mind your own business" - this kind of treatment begs the question of transparency in conservation. Both lodge managers were conspicuous by their absence at the lodge during that evening dinner. It was left to the house-keeping manager (who had accompanied us on the game drive) to inform us that; "all has been taken care of - so don't worry about it, OK."

Well, I do worry about it. Especially when no gun shots were heard that night, nor was any feedback forthcoming the following day. One has to ask the following questions:

1. Were these two animals left to suffer all night and either be taken down by the resident hyenas or butchered and carted off by the poacher?

2. What anti-poaching and snare removal efforts are made by the game reserve staff?

3. Was the lack of action due to apathy or to a lack of funds to procure the necessary animal rescue resources and tools?

From a transparency point of view, witnessing the shooting of an injured animal would clearly upset some guests, so lodge manager two's reaction is understandable in this regard. However, witnessing the rescue and release of an entangled but moderately uninjured animal is an entirely different matter.

or to Shoot Injured Wildlife?

Many game reserves that I have visited encourage their guests to participate in wire snare locating and removal while on a guided walking safari. Being actively involved in rescuing an ensnared animal would send most visitors into rapture and as tourists are prone to do, they would share their experience, images and video clips on social media pages and sing the praises of the reserve, lodge and country.

So, if allowing guests to witness an animal rescue is good for public relations, maybe the quoted reaction is about economics.

I did some quick research over the internet, which revealed that the cost of a tranquillizer dart is approximately R250.00 per dart (depending on the immobilising drug used), and roughly the same price for 500 rounds of .22 high velocity rifle bullets. By contrast, the cost of an Impala at a game auction is around R650.00.

So which was it? Did the reserve not have any tranquillizer darts and the necessary blow-gun with which to administer it? Were bullets or perhaps rifles in short supply? Or do Impala breed so rapidly that they are expendable?

The conservation officer at this particular game reserve was given an opportunity to comment on this article, and here is his reply:

"As you may know, conservation is by no means sunshine and roses, and quite often difficult decisions regarding the fate of certain animals has to be made, no matter how hard it is emotionally. To clarify as to what happened to the impala, we did in the end decide to take it out. The decisions was not an easy one, but we had to weigh up both financial and conservation reasons. To motivate, financially it would be too expensive, as yes, a dart may only cost R250, however, new laws prohibit just any person having these drugs on their property unless they are a registered vet. Even for game capture teams these days, they have to have a vet present for darting purposes due to how dangerous these drugs are to humans and also the current poaching situation within SA. Given this fact, we have to add the cost of a vet to travel to the reserve,

the cost per hour to locate the impala, which in this instance took over four hours to locate. A bill like this would easily have amounted to over R2500 for an animal worth R650.

Added to this, quite often there are other unseen internal injuries that have been caused by the snare such as blood circulation issues, and added to the stress of being darted, could also dramatically reduce the chances of survival making it a 50/50 option. An impala is by far the most successful breeder of the antelope on the property, therefore, you can understand that it was in the best interest all round to take it out of its suffering.

As for the wildebeest, the tendons inside the joint were severed and the was little hope of recovery as there is no way to keep a wild animal like this immobilised for the amount of time it would take for the leg to recover.

The reason why you would not have heard the shots is because we use a .22 calibre rifle with a silencer on, so as to not cause any further stress to the injured and surrounding animals, as is clearly visible by how calm the animals are around the lodge.

We understand that you as a guest, especially being a journalist, would really have liked to be part of an operation of this kind, but it is at the end of the day not something that we want our guests to see, or to be part of, for many reasons that we have learned over the past thirteen years of being in this industry.

Very rarely does an incident like this take a positive turn. We understand your justification on how this can have positive repercussions/snowball effect if a guest gets to experience a search and rescue kind of operation, but perception is in the eye of the beholder, and not every guest understands when tough decisions are made." t

OVERSTRAND - SOUTH AFRICA

Exploring the Cape Whale Coast

If unusual destinations and unique experiences are attributes that differentiate tour operator and travel agent success, then the **Cape Whale Coast** region of South Africa's Western Cape province should be included as it possesses both in abundance.

By **Des Langkilde**.

GPS Coordinates: 34°25'S 19°20'E

The star attraction. Hermanus ihas become known as a mecca for whale watching during the southern hemisphere winter months (June - October), when in excess of 100 whales can be in the area with their young as they come to Walker Bay to calve and TO mate. Many behaviours such as breaching, sailing, lobtailing, or spyhopping can be witnessed.

Image courtesy of www.southernrightcharters.co.za

Proteas grow abundantly among the fynbos in the Kogelberg Biosphere, Onrus Mountain Conservancy and the Fernkloof Nature Reserve.

As a publisher and travel writer, I've visited Cape Town and its wine regions on many occasions but never ventured beyond the Kogelberg mountains and over Sir Lowry's Pass to explore the Western Cape province of South Africa's **Overberg** region *(the name translated from Afrikaans, literally means 'the other side of the mountain')*. Until now, that is!

In this article, I will focus on a general overview of the Overstrand region, as the coastal towns of the Cape Whale Coast are where the majority of tourists flock. To keep this article brief, I have included hyper-links for further reading on attractions or places of interest by underlining them.

Due to Overstrand's close proximity to Cape Town *(an hour's drive East of the International airport, along the N2 freeway through Somerset West and Sir Lowry's Pass and take the Hermanus / Botrivier off-ramp)* many of the towns are holiday resorts. The municipal area of Overstrand is huge, covering a surface of almost 1708 square kilometres, which stretches along the Atlantic seaboard from Betty's Bay in the East to Gansbaai in the West, and has four tourist information centres located in **Kleinmond**, **Hermanus**, **Stanford** and **Gansbaai.** The largest town is Hermanus, which is situated on the northern edge of Walker Bay next to the Klein River mouth.

Clarence Drive

Opting for the more scenic drive from Cape Town *(along the N2, before Sir Lowry's Pass, turn right at the Gordon's Bay / Kleinmond sign and left at the T-junction in Gordon's Bay, onto the R44)*, Clarence Drive is a coastal road carved from rocky sea cliffs, which in my opinion rivals Cape Town's Chapman's Peak Drive between Noordhoek and Hout Bay in terms of scenic beauty *(and without any toll fees)*, and provides magnificent views across False Bay to Table Mountain and the Cape Peninsula. Although Clarence Drive is rather steep, there are ample lay-by view points *(sufficiently wide enough for tour coaches)*, which provide tourists with ideal photo opportunities and an ideal introduction to the region en route to their accommodation.

One of the many lay-by view points along Clarence Drive

Pringle Bay beach viewed from Clarence Drive.

Clarence Drive leads through the Kogelberg Biosphere, the first and only Biosphere in South Africa to be proclaimed by the United Nations' Educational, Scientific and Cultural Organisation (UNESCO): a testament to the stunning diversity and large number of its flowering plants, many of which are found nowhere else in the fynbos biome. The reserve boasts more than 1,880 different plant species, of which seventy seven species occur nowhere else on earth *(the next richest is the South American rainforest with just 420 species per 10,000 square kilometres)*.

The Drive leads to Kogel Bay – a surfers paradise with barrel breaks curling along an expansive stretch of white beach, favoured by topless sunbathers for its sheltered cove and protection from occasional southeaster wind.

Rooiels to Kleinmond

Rooiels is the next attraction along the Cape Whale Coast route – a small seaside village and a favourite spot for family outings on the beach. Five kilometres on is **Pringle Bay**, with quaint holiday homes along the shoreline and a few restaurants for light lunches. **Hangklip** *('hanging rock' literally named after the draping rock-face that appears to cling to the mountainside)* appears to the right of a sharp bend in the road and forms the entrance to *False Bay* with its 22 meter lighthouse tower that has kept sailors, seafarers and fisherman safe since 1960.

Driving another ten kilometres reveals **Betty's Bay** – once the site of a whaling station and home to one of only two mainland Jackass Penguin Colonies in South Africa *(the other is* Boulder's Beach *- in Simon's Town, which forms part of the* Table Mountain National Park *Marine Protected Area)*. The Harold Porter National Botanical Garden is well worth a visit and is located within the Kogelberg Biosphere Reserve. The nominal entrance fee *(see link for rates)* is worth the privilege of experiencing the garden trails, and guided group tours can be arranged by booking at least two weeks in advance.

Kleinmond, at the foot of the Palmietberg, is the next town and the Hangklip-Kleinmond Tourism Bureau is located in the Protea Centre on the left of Main Road – worth a brief stop-over to collect product brochures and view their display of local artefacts and

fynbos plant samples. The Kleinmond new harbour area is also worth a visit, where your clients can buy honey, biltong, dried fynbos flowers, and arts & crafts, or enjoy fresh oysters and line-fish at any of the several restaurants.

Organised annual events along the Hangklip-Kleinmond route include the Totalsports Challenge *(a seven discipline sporting event)* in January, the Big Blues Music Festival in March, African X Trail *(trail running)* in April, the Gravity Adventure Festival in August, the Windgat Festival *(enviro family event)* in September, and the Hot Heels Africa *(downhill skateboarding)* event in December.

From Kleinmond, the R44 road leads past the Botrivier Estuary and ends in a T-junction on the R43, where one can either to turn right towards Hermanus and the Whale Route, or turn left to explore the Elgin Valley and Overberg countryside along the N2 towards George and the Garden Route.

A view from the top of Rotary Way looking towards Hermanus, Grotto beach, the Klein River estuary and Walker Bay Nature Reserve.

Fisherhaven lagoon is an ideal location for fishing and water sports.

Fisherhaven to Hermanus

Opting for the right turn, the pristine Onrus Mountain Conservancy flanks the left side of the road as one passes by the seaside resorts of **Fisherhaven** with its lagoon, yacht club, public slipway and playground, and a herd of wild horses that have adapted to a diet of slightly saline water and plants. *(It is interesting to note that during World War II, the Royal Air Force Squadron 262 established a diversion base at the lagoon and Consolidated PBY Catalina flying boats operated from here)*, **Hawston**, which boasts an immaculate Blue Flag beach, and **Vermont** with its luxurious homes nestled amongst the fynbos or overlooking the rocky coastline. **Onrus** is the next village, which means *'restless'* in Afrikaans, referring to the pounding of the surf on the rocky coast. It is a predominantly residential area close to the coastline, as is **Sandbaai** *(Sand Bay)*, which neighbours Onrusrivier and shares a popular swimming beach.

The Old Harbour viewed from Rotary Way.

Proceeding along the R43 *(note the speed restriction signs)*, a sign posted turn-off on the left to Rotary Way leads to the top of the mountain range, giving the viewer an elevated panoramic photo opportunity of this pristine area.

Back onto the R43, the New and Old Harbour turn-off appears on the right. The Old Harbour Museum is well worth a visit. The museum comprises two sections: the Historical Old Fishing Harbour and the Fisherman's Village that displays boats, the old sea wall, brine tanks and *'bokkom'* (salted fish) stands. The indoor museum houses a photographic exhibition of Old Hermanus, which dates back as far as the end of the 19th Century and beginning of the 20th.

Continuing along the R43, the road leads into **Hermanus** *(originally called Hermanuspietersfontein, but shortened as the name was too long for the postal service)*, which is the commercial hub of the Overstrand and is famous for southern right whale watching during winter and spring *(June to September)* - hence the Overstrand's marketing slogan: **'The Whale Coast'**. Whales were once hunted in Betty's Bay, but are now protected to ensure the survival of the species. The Old Harbour Museum contains several exhibitions that explain the whaling industry, and the De Wetshuis Photo Museum houses an exhibition of photos that depict the history of Hermanus. The Whale Museum houses a skeleton of a whale and shows an audio-visual presentation of whales and dolphins twice daily.

Hermanus has the world's only Whale Crier, whose job is to blow his kelp horn thus announcing where whales have been spotted. His calls can also be heard during tours, as tour groups visit several of the more well known areas for whale watching and are told the related history of Hermanus. The current Whale Crier is Eric Davalah, who out of season can be found at either the Information Kiosk at the Village Square or at the Hermanus Tourism Bureau in Mitchell Street.

Besides it's reputation as a whale watching destination, Hermanus is also one of the few municipalities that taken accessible tourism seriously by providing demarcated areas with 'Disabled Friendly' logo signage. Bathrooms for disabled visitors can be found at the

The Whale Crier of Hermanus - Eric Davalah

Grotto Beach in Hermanus, showing the beach-friendly wheelchairs

Market Square and Municipal Library, whilst recreational facilities where the disabled can be accommodated are at the Village Craft Market, Fernkloof Nature Reserve, certain parts of the Cliff Paths, Voëlklip beach, the Public Library, the Cliff Top Development and Grotto Beach. *Note: for helpful hints on catering to the needs of disabled tourists, read the QASA 'Sawubona Disability' booklet for Myths, Manners, Do's & Don'ts about Disability.*

Popular attractions in Hermanus include the 1800 hectare Fernkloof Nature Reserve, the Hemel-en-Aarde Valley – a 6.7 kilometre Wine Route along the R320 to Caledon, Gearing's Point and the Cliff Paths, which offer one of the best locations for whale spotting and watching, and the Blue Flag Grotto Beach, which stretches for almost 18 kilometres, fronting the Klein River lagoon and Walker Bay Nature Reserve, and has two beach-friendly wheelchairs in place for those with physical disabilities to access the sea.

Hermanus is also home to SANSA Space Science, formerly known as the Hermanus Magnetic Observatory. SANSA Space Science is the warning centre for Africa, one of thirteen regional warning centres around the world, which monitor extreme space weather and solar magnetic activity.

Annual events in Hermanus include the FynArts Festival (June), the Kalfiefees and Food and Wine Festival (Hermanuspietersfontein) in August, the Whale Festival and the Flower Festival (BOTSOC) in September.

Stanford to Gansbaai

Driving through Hermanus along the R43, the village of **Stanford** lies inland, about a 20 minute drive from Hermanus. This quaint historic village is ideal for day trippers looking for antique stores, restaurants, vineyards, coffee shops or a picnic in the country. Stanford is fast becoming a food destination with chefs serving an array of fresh and locally produced food with a leaning towards the slow food movement. Foods range from family fare, gourmet delights, country comfort cuisine, and pub grub to fine dining.

Continuing along the R43, the Grootbos Nature Reserve rises against fynbos clad hills above Walker Bay with breathtaking views of dunes, sea and the distant Cape of Good Hope. Within this eco-

paradise, lies the Grootbos Private Nature Reserve with two 5-Star luxury lodges, a Villa, consisting of six elegant suites accommodating up to 12 guests, and two fully equipped spa facilities *(read our Property Review here, and our Grootbos Eco-tourism Case Study here).*

De Kelders ('The Caves' in Afrikaans) is the next turn-off. De Kelders is a residential area and in spite of its reputation as a premium whale watching site, it has been immune to large scale tourism developments. There is a restaurant, bakery and pub in De Kelders as well as a coffee shop overlooking the bay. De Kelders has several guesthouses and B&B's of which many are situated right on the cliffs overlooking the ocean.

Gansbaai is the next town along this stretch of the Cape Whale Coast. The town of Gansbaai is the business hub of the area, with a number of restaurants and a commercial fishing harbour. The Danger Point Lighthouse is situated on the Gansbaai peninsula, which is a rock reef that extends for about 8km out to sea. A hidden rock lurks just below the surface off the Point, and it is this rock that the legendary HMS Birkenhead collided with in 1852. Seven shipwrecks surround Danger Point and 140 wrecks are dotted along the shores between Danger Point and Cape Infanta.

Blompark is located in the heart of the Gansbaai area, surrounded by fynbos vegetation and only a short walk on the gravel road to **Romansbaai**, traditionally the beach for the people of Blompark. Many of the inhabitants of Blompark are descendants of the earliest residents of the Gansbaai area. Up to 40 years ago, the community now living in Blompark had their traditional home more or less immediately on the doorstep of Romansbaai, next to the old municipal stores, called the "Old Location". Today the Blompark people call their former home the "Nets Court" to pay tribute to the fishing tradition that was established there.

Kleinbaai, on the eastern side of Gansbaai is the launch site for white shark cage diving, which takes between 3-5 hours, depending on the weather, sea conditions and shark behaviour. Trips depart from Kleinbaai harbour and the anchor site depends on the sea conditions, weather and previous shark sightings. Tourists wishing to cage dive do not have to be scuba qualified. Weather permitting, White Shark cage diving and sightseeing tours run daily, however prime viewing time is in the South African winter months when the sharks have a particularly active feeding pattern. The following guide is based on observations by

The boat launch site at Kleinbaai, which has earned Gansbaai its reputaion as the 'Great White Shark Capital of the World™'.

White Shark Projects over the past eight years. Allow for an overlap between seasons:

- Peak season: April to October (99% success rate).
- High season: November to December (90 – 99% success rate).
- Intermediate season: January to March (80 – 90% success rate).

Water temperatures vary between 12 and 20 degrees Celsius during peak and high season and between 10 and 16 degrees Celsius during intermediate season.

Dyer Island, located a few kilometres out to sea south of Gansbaai, is a protected bird sanctuary and hosts a large colony of African Penguins - about 25 000 pairs. Today, there are only about 900 penguin pairs left due to human interference This small, twenty hectare island is the easternmost of the chain of seabird islands off the Western Cape.

Rare, endangered bird species such as the Roseate Tern and the Leach's Storm Petrel still breed on Dyer island, as well as seabirds such as the Whitebreasted, Cape, Bank and Crowned Cormorants, Kelp Gulls and Hartlaub's Gulls, and Swift Terns. Huge roosts of terns, mainly the migratory Common and Sandwich Terns, occur in summer. Antarctic Terns, which breed on the sub-antarctic islands, roost here in winter.

Dyer Island is a nature reserve managed by CapeNature, but has no visitor access facilities. This is understandable both in terms of the sensitivity of the island's birds to disturbance, and because it is very tricky to reach. The best landing place on the island can only be used in fairly calm conditions. Many people (including scientists) have been stranded there, waiting for the weather to clear!

Adjacent to Dyer Island is **Geyser Rock**, where a colony of 60 000 Cape Fur Seals breed. The strip of sea between Dyer Island and Geyser Rock is aptly dubbed 'Shark Alley', as the seals who feed here are a constant food source to the sharks. During winter months *(May to August)*, the alley is a hub of activity when many young seal pups end up as easy, juicy shark meals.

The area around Dyer Island and Shark Alley is ideal for shark cage diving and provides excellent sightings of shark breaching and predation. It is an amazing experience to watch a Great White leap right out of the water to ambush a seal. This is the reason why Gansbaai is known as the 'Great White Shark Capital of the World™'.

Franskraal to Die Dam

Franskraal, a short drive up from Kleinbaai, is a seaside village boasting a safe swimming beach and is a botanist's dream. The signposted 'Groot Melkhoutbos Trail' provides a lovely meander through a Milkwood forest. The historical Strandveld Museum on the beachfront of Franskraal, has the largest collection of relics of the HMS Birkenhead. The owners are local historians and marvellous story tellers who will gladly conduct tours for a trip through time.

Baardskeerdersbos forms part of the Gansbaai municipal region and is located inland *(turnoff on the left of the R43 before Uilenkraalsmond)*. Baardskeerdersbos Valley is one of the most undisturbed and original areas of the Overberg. The village apparently gets its name from the small spider-like Solifugae arachnids known as *Baardscheerders* (Beard Shavers), which purportedly cut human hair for nest-making purposes. The first mention of Baardskeerdersbos is to be found in a report-back to Jan van Riebeeck in 1660 by an expedition team of five men who reported on the village and its Khoikhoi residents. The newly formed Art-Route invites visitors into the homes of artists and crafters on certain weekends of the year.

Uilenkraalsmond follows Franskraal and is situated at the mouth of the Uilenkraal River. This is a very popular holiday resort with a modern caravan park, supertube, putt-putt course, trampoline and pub. Its tranquil lagoon is safe for swimming and tourists can enjoy long walks on the beach.

Pearly Beach is next on the R43 Cape Whale Coast Route. This is a small, laid back seafront village, where the main attraction is seemingly endless, white, unspoilt beaches. In spring *(August-October)*, the wild flowers are quite spectacular. Among the variety of bird life, twitchers will find the endangered Black African Oystercatcher and the Cape Sugar Bird. Some of these can be seen in the Fynbos garden that has been established, and along the interpretive beach walks whilst exploring the shoreline ecology.

After Pearly Beach, the R43 to the east mysteriously ends in the middle of nowhere. It does not even continue with a dirt-track.

Shark bait: Cape fur seals flourish on Dire Island and Geyser Rock (in case you're wondering, the sign has been superimposed - it's actually located in Kleinbaai).

This road to nowhere ends exactly at the eastern extreme of the Gansbaai area.

However, if you turn right towards the sea a few kilometres before the end of the road to nowhere, you end up at a secluded spot on the beach, known as **Buffeljagsbaai** (Buffalo-hunt bay). It is a small settlement of one street and a bit. The residents live off the sea as they always have. Buffeljagsbaai is neither a place of luxury nor of facilities for the day-visitor, yet its raw beauty and seclusion makes it an attraction in itself.

On the other side of Buffeljagsbaai is **Jessie se Baai** (Jessie's Bay), named after the ship of the same name that was wrecked here. The impressive solidified sand dunes towering over the beach are the reason that the locals know this place by another name: Die hohe walle (The high walls).

The end of Jessie se Baai is where the land-mass of **Quoin Point** begins. Quoin Point is the second most southern point of the African continent and one of the most densely packed shipwreck graves of the South African coast. Quoin Point is devoid of man-made things, apart from a small light tower and few fishing cottages owned by the Schipper and October families of Elim. These families were granted the right of use of this small peninsula by Queen Victoria. After the wreckage of yet another English ship, the English government thought it was a good idea to have people living here permanently. The document granting this right to the respective Elim-people was signed by Queen Victoria herself.

Die Dam, is a popular fishing spot and forms the absolute end of the R43, and hence the end of the Cape Whale Coast route.

Tourist Guides

Of course, the Cape Whale Coast is best experienced with the knowledgeable raconteuring of a registered tourist guide. Local guides can be sourced by contacting one of the Tourism Bureaus (see links below) or by searching for a member on the Cape Tourist Guides Association website.

Conclusion

It is apparent from this article that the Overberg region, and specifically the Overstrand (Cape Whale Coast) has an abundance of natural attractions and a vast array of accommodation establishments to suit all travel budget requirements. Whilst I have attempted to visit as many attractions along the Cape Whale Coast route as possible, I have only scratched the surface. 🌐

Links:

Accommodation in Pringle Bay, Betty's Bay & Rooi Els: www.baytown.co.za

Accommodation website for members of the Hermanus Tourism Bureau: www.whalecoast.info

Business Directory and Tourism Portal for the Overberg: www.hermanus.co.za

Gansbaai Tourism Bureau: www.gansbaaiinfo.com

Hermanus Tourism Bureau: www.hermanusaccommodation.co.za

Hangklip - Kleinmond Tourism Bureau: www.ecoscape.org.za

Official website of the Cape Whale Coast Destination Marketing Organisation: www.overberg.co.za

Overstrand Municipality: www.overstrand.gov.za

Stanford Tourism Bureau: www.stanfordinfo.co.za

Sunsets are the coup de grâce of the Cape Whale Coast and precede another attraction on cloudless nights - namely star gazing, which is maginfied by the 'Champaign Air' of Hermanus.

Quality Control In
EVENTS MANAGEMENT

By **Beaulah du Toit**.

This article reviews the steps needed to maintain consistent quality through project management principles that are the hallmark of successful events.

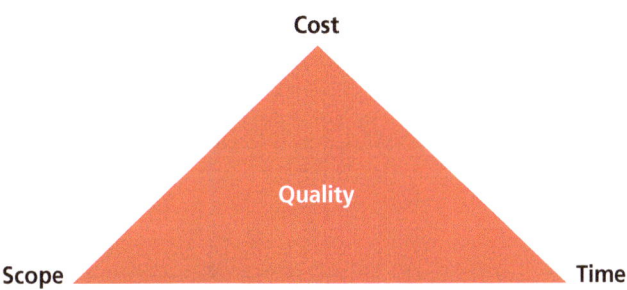

The classic project management triangle clearly indicates that failure or reduction of any one of the factors of scope, time and cost compromises quality. To reduce this risk, attention must be paid to each one of these factors at the beginning of the events management project.

Scope

The majority of projects suffer from scope 'creep' and this not only affects the quality but also can severely influence the cost of an event. To reduce this, the scope of the event must be clearly defined at the onset of the project. The client's brief is the single most important document in events management, yet too often, it is not clearly articulated or even recorded.

Part of this can relate to the client's vague terms of reference or brief – most people simply see the polished delivery of a first class event, without being aware of the amount of effort required to produce such an event, similar to an audience's unawareness of the backstage of a theatre production. Part of this can also be attributed to a failure on the part of the events manager to elicitate all aspects of an event, according to an established project plan.

At this stage, the events manager can advise the client on programme constraints, financial risks and implications, price dynamics and risk management factors that will add to costs. The element of availability and time constraints of people and material can be fully explored up front.

Time

Internationally, events are planned anywhere from 1-4 years in advance and this allows for better pricing deals and extensive Gantt charts, detailing every aspect of the event. However, events are often suddenly required – because of a need to use up allocated budget or because the client has realised, quite far into the project, that professional help is required.

When time is squeezed, it can become difficult to produce a quality event. The most appropriate venue may not be available; the top entertainers may be booked; the keynote speaker in the subject may be unobtainable etc. Professional events managers can work around short project cycles but this affects costs, if the quality is to be maintained.

Cost

Poor budgeting is one of the key reasons why events fail to reach the expected quality.

A major misconception about events management costs is that an event can pay for itself at its conclusion or that 'free' events only need be settled 30 days after the event. However, most venues require at least 50% deposit for a booking, as do the secondary suppliers of food, drinks, audio-visual equipment and entertainers. Without these deposits, no event can be guaranteed.

This means requires the events management company create a payment plan, where tranches are made according to project phases. This can only be done if there is an official signed order and an understanding that this 'banking' privilege carries additional costs, as the events management company is at risk for several months leading up to the events and possibly another 60 days later.

Conclusion

A winning event is the combination of a professional events management team, fully versed in all aspects of project management, and the knowledgeable client, who understands that events require expert input to achieve winning outputs.

About the author: Beaulah du Toit is the Operations & Logistics Director of Litha Communications. Email: Beaulah@lithacommunications.co.za or visit www.lithacommunications.co.za

THE METRIC
(That Most Hoteliers Ignore)

By **Jean Francois Mourier**.

That Can Significantly Impact Your Revenues

When most hoteliers consider their revenue management metrics, they most likely think about RevPAR, ADR and occupancy. Perhaps, they would also think about historical and current local demand.

But for the majority of hoteliers, their property's star rating wouldn't even occur to them (beyond when they initially start working with an OTA and are creating their profile).

What many hoteliers forget is that a property's star rating is a hugely important factor, both in marketing your property and in determining the best price for your rooms on a given day – because consumers often use star ratings to filter viewing search results on an OTA.

By now, most hoteliers are probably familiar with the Cornell University study, which offered quantifiable proof that having a better TripAdvisor rating would help boost a property's bottom line; the study showed that:

"… a 1-percent increase in a hotel's online reputation score leads up to a 0.89-percent increase in price as measured by the hotel's average daily rate (ADR). Similarly this 1-percent increase in reputation also leads to an occupancy increase of up to 0.54 percent. Finally, this 1-percent reputation improvement leads up to a 1.42-percent increase in revenue per available room (RevPAR)[1]".

The same applies to the impact of your property's star rating on your room rate. Let's look at an example of a three-star, 100-room hotel in the United States, which earns $110 of RevPAR per room, per day; if the same property went up to a three and half-star rating, their RevPAR would increase

by $42 per room, per day. If you extrapolate those numbers, the property can increase their annual revenues by approx. $1.5million, simply by increasing their star rating by one half-star (from three-stars to three-and-half-stars)!

As you can see, star ratings *do* have a direct impact on your property's bottom line.

Even still, some hoteliers are hesitant to try to improve their star rating because they believe that (with a higher star rating), potential customers will have much greater expectations about their property. They operate under the philosophy: "Under-promise, over-deliver," because they think it will be better, both financially and for customer satisfaction rates, to be the best hotel in a lower star rating (rather than one of many in the higher rating). But that isn't always true.

It is true that, from a consumer standpoint, a higher rating is perceived to be a "better" property; however, not all travelers use the same criteria for judgement so "better" is a very subjective term. Some customers would perceive a hotel with more amenities to be "better" (and therefore, worth a higher star rating); whereas, others might perceive a clean hotel with interesting design choices to be "better" in a good location (and therefore, worth a higher rating). The point is that you can't always please every customer, no matter your star rating; however, by having a higher star rating, you're more likely to secure more, higher priced bookings.

So what now? Focus on optimizing your actual star rating on the most popular, top-performing OTAs in your region (i.e. Expedia in the North America, Booking.com in Europe, Agoda in Asia, etc.). Since this is the site that brings you the majority of your OTA business, the effort you put into increasing your star rating (on this site) will be a worthwhile investment. Keep in mind though, like every other aspect of the online channels, chaos reigns supreme. Many properties will likely have different star ratings on different OTAs, because each site uses different criteria to determine their ratings.

Additionally, you want to make sure you review your comp set's star rating so that you can know if your property has an advantage (making it more valuable to the customer) or a disadvantage (which would entice customers to book elsewhere).

And finally, I recommend that all properties use a sophisticated revenue management system (RMS) to make executing their strategy easier and less time-consuming. A sophisticated RMS will monitor your property's and your competitors' star rating on the important channels - as well as the performance of your competitors and market conditions - on an ongoing basis, and then adjust your pricing accordingly. It will collect and analyze data constantly, and will continuously adapt to increase your property's revenues without you lifting a finger.

See, isn't that so much easier?!

About the Author: Jean Francois Mourier is the CEO of REVPAR GURU - an alternative revenue management software solution, designed to deliver maximum bookings and profits. For more information visit www.revparguru.com

[1] http://scholarship.sha.cornell.edu/chrpubs/5/

Night Shift, Employees and Transportation

When overtime and night work overlap, are employees entitled to transportation?

By **Fiona Leppan**.

Night shifts raise concerns, especially about the safety of employees and the transport available to employees who perform night work. Although section 17(2)(b) of the Basic Conditions of Employment Act, No 75 of 1997 (BCEA) requires suitable transport to be available for night shift workers, it does not explain whether an employee who works overtime beyond 18h00 is also entitled to such transport. This question was dealt with by the Labour Appeal Court (LAC) in TFD Network Africa (Pty) Ltd v Singh NO and Others (LAC: PA 16/15).

In this case, the employee was contractually required to work overtime as and when his employer required. The terms and conditions of his employment were regulated by the BCEA and National Bargaining Council Agreement of the Bargaining Council for the Road Freight Industry of 2004 (Agreement).

The employee's shift ended at 17:00 but he was instructed by this employer to work overtime until 19:00. He however only worked until 18:00. His explanation was that there was a lack of transport to his home. He also explained that although there was a bus that left at 19:15, after getting off the bus, he was required to walk about two kilometres to his home and he stated that it was not safe to walk around his neighbourhood at that time of night.

He was later dismissed for breach of contract and for refusing to obey a reasonable instruction. The employee argued that in terms of the BCEA, public transport was required to be available for night shift workers.

The employee challenged his dismissal. The employer argued that the employee did not perform night work on the basis that the majority of his shift was not worked within the hours 18:00 and 06:00. The arbitrator

found that the employee's dismissal was unfair. The employer took the arbitrator's decision on review to the Labour Court. The Labour Court did not review and set aside the award. The employer then took the matter on appeal to the LAC.

The employer raised various arguments, in essence, relating to the fact that the work performed by the employee was not night work and that the employee was not entitled to refuse the instruction to work overtime. In particular, the employer argued inter alia that the majority of the shift must fall between 18:00 and 6:00 to constitute night work and "overtime work following on a normal working shift that ends before 18:00, that resorts within the hours of 18:00 to 06:00 does not constitute night work".

The LAC considered the provisions of the Agreement and held that the night work definition and transport obligations mirrored those set out in the BCEA. In terms of the

Agreement, an employer could only require an employee to perform night work if transportation was available between the workplace and the employee's home when the employee's shift started and ended.

The LAC held that it is clear that in terms of the Agreement all work performed between 18:00 and 06:00 is night work regardless of whether it is overtime or not. However, work performed on a regular basis between 23:00 and 06:00 attracts further obligations.

The LAC rejected the argument that the majority of the shift comprised a day shift because whether it is overtime or regular work, work performed between 18:00 and 06:00 constitutes night work. The requirement of available transport exists once an employee works beyond 18:00, regardless of whether it is an overtime or actual night shift.

About the Author: Fiona Leppan is a Director in Cliffe Dekker Hofmeyr's Employment Practice.

Extra Public Holiday this December

This year 25 December 2016 falls on a Sunday. This means that the following Monday, 26 December 2016 will also be a public holiday. However, 26 December 2016 is Goodwill Day and already a public holiday in terms of the Public Holidays Act, No 36 of 1994 (Act). President Zuma has declared Tuesday, 27 December to be an additional public holiday.

Questions arise as to whether an employer is obliged to pay an employee for the Sunday and Monday or only one of these days. The legal position in this regard is as follows:

If an employee works on a public holiday, the employer must consider the provisions of the Basic Conditions of Employment Act, No 75 of 1997 (BCEA) when determining the

amount to pay the employee. In particular, the employer must consider whether the public holiday falls on a day on which the employee would ordinarily work. If so, then the employee is entitled to double his/her ordinary wage for the day or, if greater, the employee's ordinary wage for the day "plus the amount earned by the employee for the time worked on that day". However, if the employee does not work on the public holiday which falls on a day the employee would ordinarily work, the employee is entitled to his/her ordinary wage for the day.

The same applies in respect of Sunday, 1 January 2017 where both that day together with the following Monday are deemed to be public holidays.

FROM THE

BENCH™

With Louis the Lawyer
BENCHMARK ©

RISK IN TOURISM

THE LAW: CONTRACTS

- Part 24 -

Signature

The Role of: Service Level Agreements

Service level agreements ('SLA') come in different guises and fulfil varied functions.

The SLA is mainly uses in two ways – it is either a *'stand-alone'* agreement or it forms part of/is an addendum to an agreement. It should be borne in mind that whatever the format (if properly drafted) it is a proper binding agreement giving rise to enforceable rights and obligations.

If it is a *'stand-alone'* agreement, it is imperative that all elements be addressed i.e. not only service delivery but also issues such as term and termination, liability, dispute, etc. The service delivery should address the expectations and deliverables of each party and are usually referred to as *'Key Performance Areas'* ('KPA') and *'Key Performance Indicators'* ('KPI'). When it is an addendum, only the KPA and KPI need to be addressed.

However what is very often not done in whichever format the SLA is used is to link the KPI to breach, the very purpose of the SLA. By linking the two it makes the identification of breaches that much easier, takes it out of the subjective realm and can not only be linked to issues such as penalties but also early termination.

What are the benefits of an SLA?
- Manages & identifies expectations of the parties
- Provides framework to manage relationship
- Creates an awareness of the impact of poor service
- Identifies each party's needs and obligations resulting in organised goals
- This in turn leads to goal orientated controls
- Stimulates constant improvement
- Promotes: Communication/understanding/teamwork

The SLA is a dynamic document and should be linked to the following:

- Audits
- Reviews
- Customer satisfaction surveys
- Help desk reports
- Management reports

Thus the SLA must be addressed in the process of deciding whether or not to litigate and if so the role of the SLA. If it has been effectively and unequivocally drafted, it can be a very useful dispute resolution mechanism. The non-compliance with some KPI can have concomitant penalties whereas others may give the affected party the right to terminate.

DECISION TIME: LITIGATE OR SETTLE?

We have over the past few months given you an outline of issues to consider and possible strategies and now it is up to you – remember:

- Assess all matters & weigh up implications
- Make the right commercial decision – against legal 'backdrop'
- Your final decision must NOT be driven by (outside) legal representation
- Bear in mind ALL the implications of litigation
- Always bear in mind the *'grapevine'* (rumours) – effective, early and ongoing communications are crucial!!!

Next year we will discuss the various alternatives to litigation – **have a super Festive Season!**

This series of articles explores the legal aspects associated with the risks of operating an adventure tourism business, with specific relevance to the legal framework applicable to South Africa.

Part 1 can be read online HERE, **Part 2** HERE, **Part 3** HERE, **Part 4** HERE, and **Part 5** HERE.

Part 6

ADVENTURE TOURISM from a legal perspective

By 'Louis The Lawyer'

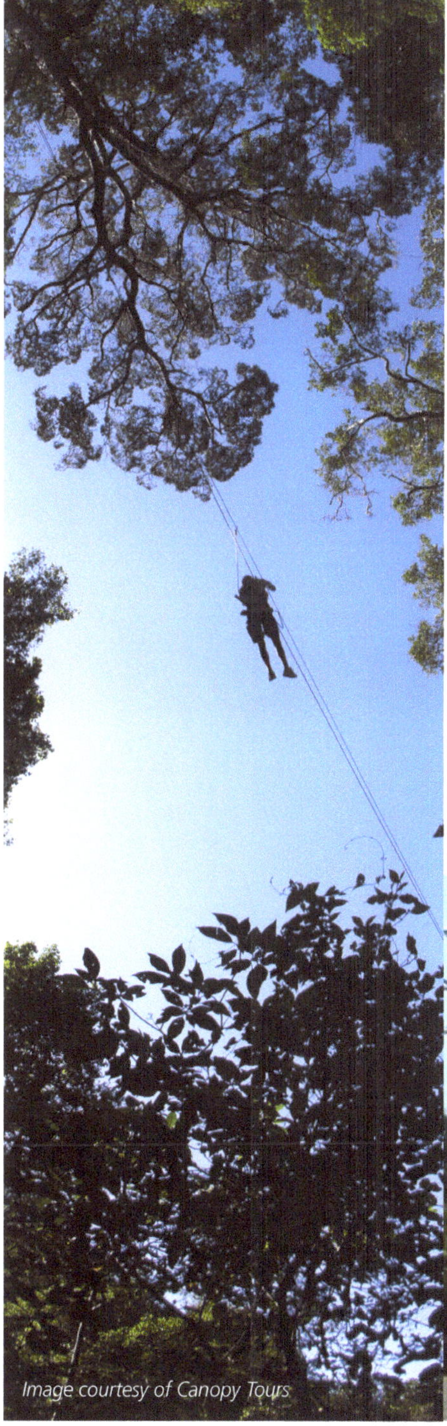

Image courtesy of Canopy Tours

Summary

Part 1 provided definitions for the term Adventure, while Part 2 looked at risk in terms of Nationality of Participant, Service Providers, Bookings, and Terms & Conditions, and Part 3 covered Indemnity and Requirements of the CPA, Part 4 explained why signage must go in hand with a sound indemnity and waiver form, and Part 5 dealt with Duty of Care in relation to Negligence, Omission, and Relationship.

DUTY OF CARE (Continued)

Acceptance of Risk

A further principle that may be applicable is that of voluntary acceptance of risk (*Volenti non fit injuria* – 'voluntary acceptance of risk does not give risk to liability').

This goes hand in hand with knowledge: of the product or service provider and the manner in which that has been imparted to, understood and accepted by the consumer/passenger (pax.)

The Consumer Protection Act (CPA) is very specific about issues such as a misapprehension on the part of the pax so it is a good idea, especially when it comes to adventure sport or 'tricky destinations' to have a comprehensive checklist and get the pax to sign it once the discussion has been completed – I would recommend in that regard the application of my CTP ('Critical Transactional Path') concept i.e. going through the anticipated trip and/or activity from start to finish so as to avoid skipping/omitting any aspect.

The management of this risk goes had in hand with a number of things:
(1) comprehensive risk management;
(2) travel policy;
(3) terms and conditions;
(4) indemnities and;
(5) insurance.

INSURANCE

As mentioned it should be in your favour when you negotiate premiums to have a combination of the above i.e. risk management, T&C and indemnities in place.

You may well be able to negotiate a lower premium and/or higher deductible if you have all of this in place.

Discuss your entire risk profile with a reputable broker and do not cut corners – pennywise = pound foolish!

To be continued in Part 7.

Disclaimer: *This article is intended to provide a brief overview of legal matters pertaining to the tadventure tourism industry and is not intended as legal advice. © Adv Louis Nel, 'Louis The Lawyer', December 2016.*

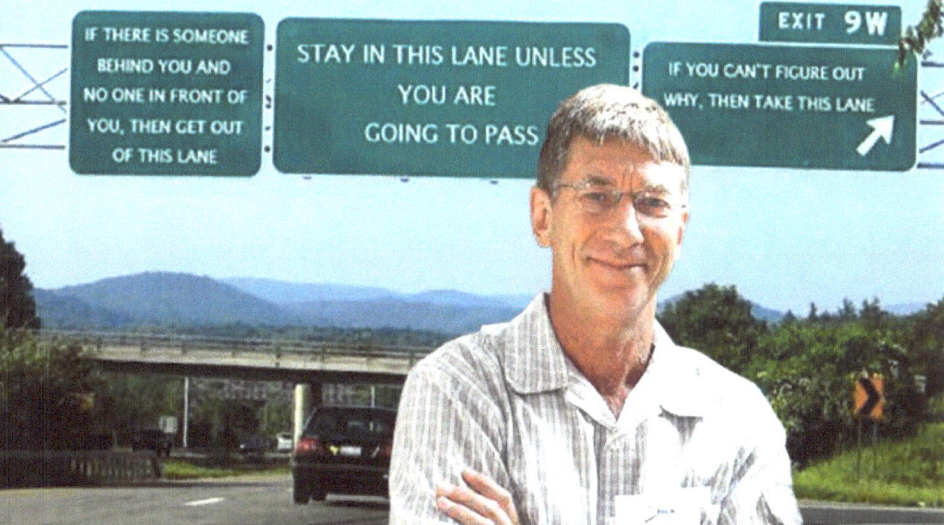

IF THERE IS SOMEONE BEHIND YOU AND NO ONE IN FRONT OF YOU, THEN GET OUT OF THIS LANE
STAY IN THIS LANE UNLESS YOU ARE GOING TO PASS
EXIT 9W
IF YOU CAN'T FIGURE OUT WHY, THEN TAKE THIS LANE

Nicholas Barenblatt, Group Marketing Manager of Protea Hotels by Marriott and African Pride Hotels

Who is the South African MILLENNIAL?

Are today's travellers really that different from their parents? What do we really know about the South African millennial traveller? Nicholas Barenblatt, of Protea Hotels by Marriott® and African Pride Hotels, provides the answers.

By **Bonny Feldman**.

As distinct trends emerge among the people that make up a business's market, marketers must take note of the trends and create products and services that tap into those trends. Failure to do so can well lead to the demise of the business. Former giants in the mobile phone industry, Nokia and Blackberry, are perfect examples of this: both have lost significant market share because they failed to innovate when buyers were looking for new technology and advanced mobile services.

"We have been very conscious of this at Protea Hotels throughout our history," explains Nicholas Barenblatt, Group Marketing Manager at Protea Hotels by Marriott® and African Pride Hotels. "It's one of the factors that made us attractive to the global hospitality giant, Marriott International, which bought Protea Hotels in 2014."

"We are at a stage now where our focus is on the millennial generation: people in their 20s and early 30s," Barenblatt explains. "This segment is critical to us because they are our new market for the next few decades, so we need to evolve our brand experience to cater for their preferences."

Research suggests that there are some distinct habits true of this generation. They are certainly more focused on the use of technology and social media than any previous generation. "Research from all over the world highlights this, and we see it among South African millennials too," Barenblatt continues. "However, one differentiating factor is the extent of access to technology. Whereas having a Notebook and a smartphone is de rigueur for our younger guests from the UK, USA, Europe and China, not all the South Africans have as much technology available. The fact that data is very costly and, coupled with internet, is not yet widely available in our country is also clear from the reaction to the free Wi-fi we offer in our hotels: whereas for foreign guests, Wi-fi is a given, many of our local guests are quite enthusiastic about the prospect of connectivity that won't cost them a fortune."

Barenblatt is also cautious about the risk of viewing millennials as a monolithic group. "In the South African context, one cannot ignore the realities of differing income brackets. The disparity between wealth and poverty is huge so we cannot view this generation as the same across the board." The same is true of levels of education. Millennials from many countries are the most highly educated generation ever. Falling university throughput rates in South Africa reveal a different scenario for this country. "Ultimately, this could impact the size of the South African millennial travel market since the country's growing skills shortages will mean that fewer local people will work in jobs that give them the means to travel," Barenblatt cautions.

Where luxury travel is concerned, the South African millennial market is relatively small compared to its foreign counterpart. In fact, we still see the higher income level groups in South Africa being skewed towards people over the age of 35, i.e. non-millennials. "This is likely to change, though," Barenblatt points out, "since these people will move into the job roles carrying big incomes as the years go by. We are also likely to see this change if we start experiencing economic growth in the country."

As for other features of millennials internationally, Barenblatt's experience points to the same health-consciousness seen internationally. People ask about healthy food options, and the hotel company has seen a demand for healthy activities. Responding to this need, some hotels are providing more healthy activities, such as mountain biking and jogging, for options over and above the usual hotel gym.

"Business must understand the target market," Barenblatt concludes. "It's what we focus on at Protea Hotels by Marriott."

PREFERENCES *of* BUSINESS TRAVELLER *Generations*

Older, experienced business travellers expect to be treated like VIPs when they travel and leave the handling of their travel arrangements to others, while younger, newer business travellers book their own travel and like to be treated like locals.

By **Lee-Ann Collingridge**.

In a global study on the preferences of the different generations of business travellers, **FCM Travel Solutions** found that travellers who are "Baby Boomers" are very aware of their status and demand that it be acknowledged by service providers. Baby boomers are aged between 56 and 71 and comprise just under a third of all business travellers (32%).

As a result, Baby Boomers fly business or first class and demand priority check-in, access to business lounges, preferred seating on aeroplanes and to be chauffeur-driven.

The study was intended to help businesses structure their travel policies to cater to the different needs of different generations of travellers and ensure better compliance.

The research found that Generation X travellers, who are aged between 36 and 55 and who constitute over half - 53% - of all business travellers, share a lot of traits with Baby Boomers.

Generation X business travellers also demand priority check-in, access to business lounges and preferred seating, but unlike their older counterparts, they tend to fly economy class and prefer to book online rather than use a travel management consultant.

They also like to extend their trips for leisure when possible - unlike Baby Boomers who maximise work by flying overnight and staying only as long as is necessary. Baby Boomers also expect a generous on-board baggage allowance.

Generation X business travellers prize relaxation, wanting breakfast to be included in their accommodation and kicking back with a drink at the end of the day.

By contrast, Generation Y business travellers - who are aged between 21 and 35 - are easygoing.

Generation Y, who constitute only 15% of business travellers, are comfortable with the sharing economy, - such as using Uber rather than being chauffeur-driven - and rather than preferred seating or lounge access, want a gym or spa at their hotel.

About the Author: *Lee-Ann Collingridge is an account director at* Flow Communications. *FCM Travel Solutions is Flight Centre Travel Group's corporate travel management company.*

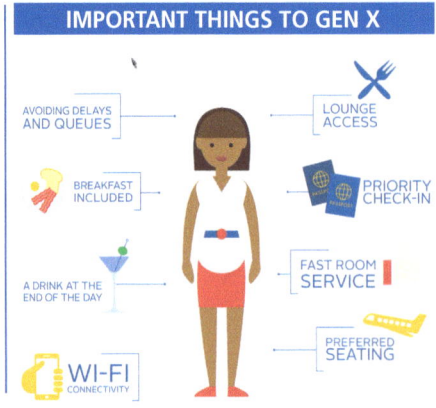

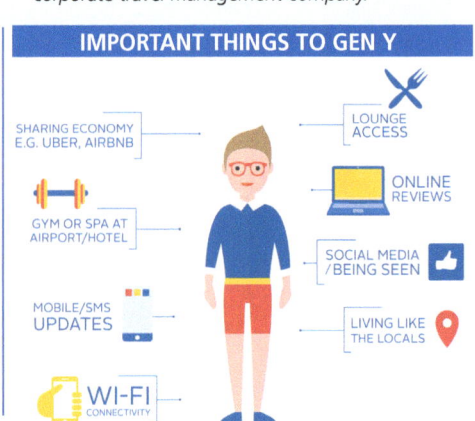

Road Trip Tips for the
HOLIDAY SEASON

The South African holiday season is around the corner and the open road is calling. Here are some road trip tips to ensure that you reach your local holiday destination safely.

By **Sharney Nel**.

Image: Chapmans Peak, Cape Town courtesy of SA Tourism.

Unfortunately, the holiday season is also the most risky time to be on the road, with an increase of car accidents that result in injuries, fatalities and also unforeseen costs. At the start of 2016, the Department of Transport reported an increase in festive season fatalities of 14% compared to the year before[1]. The festive season period usually starts from the 1st of December until the 11th of January. A recent report showed a road accident increase of 33% for the Western Cape while KwaZulu-Natal was the only province that reported a decrease compared to the previous year.

We all know the usual road safety tips to reduce the risk of an accident; do a full check-up and service your car before the trip, don't drink and drive, don't speed, keep a safe following distance, stop and rest if you get tired. But what about the not-so-obvious tips?

If you have opted to take the scenic route by going on a road trip for your local holiday this year, here are some unusual safety tips to consider before you take on the long road:

Avoid a Sugar Rush

Many people think that sugary treats, energy drinks, coffee and junk food keep their energy levels up during a road trip. This is however short-lived as you will crash soon after consuming these treats and it puts you at risk of becoming fatigued sooner. Ensure that you eat healthy snacks during your trip and drink plenty of water[2].

Activate/Change Your Voicemail Message During Your Trip

Using cellphones whilst driving is one of the major causes of accidents. People awaiting your arrival are usually curious about your whereabouts and will call to find out whether everything is all right. Change your voicemail at each rest stop to inform people of where you are in your journey and let them know where your next stop will be. This will put them (as well as yourself) at ease and avoid unnecessary phone calls during your drive.

Switch Insurance

It may not seem like a good idea to change insurance just before you go on holiday, but according to Derek Wilson, Head of Hippo.co.za, this is actually the best time to consider checking whether your insurance has you covered since you are alert and thinking of all possible scenarios, so you are able to ask all the right questions. For example, just before a trip people will question whether they have the best roadside assistance as part of their vehicle insurance cover in case of an emergency. Check and confirm that you are adequately insured by visiting Hippo.co.za to compare Car Insurance quotes from a range of South African providers.

*Based on 2016 independent market research conducted by Kaufman Levin Associates. Sources: 1. Arrive Alive; 2. News.com.

About the Author: Sharney Nel *is the Public Relations Manager at Hippo Comparative Services (Pty) Ltd – an authorised financial services provider (FSP number: 16357). Established in 2007, Hippo.co.za is South Africa's leading comparison website that helps consumers save money by comparing a range of South African providers across financial products such as Car Insurance, Household Insurance, Life Insurance, Medical Aid and more. For more information visit www.hippo.co.za*

www.ingramcontent.com/pod-product-compliance
Lightning Source LLC
Chambersburg PA
CBHW050410180526
45159CB00005B/2216